1079

Blairmore COLEMAN M

D0788521

Date Due

NOV 5 1987 DEC 3 1982		
SEP 25 '89		
MAR 4 '93		
JUN 29 63		
JUL 22 3		
MAY 25 98		
JAN 10 02		
MAY 2 3 2012		
2012		
NOV 2 8 2014		
MAY 2 6 2016		

The Boys who Saved The Children

Margaret Baldwin

JULIAN MESSNER · NEW YORK

JFM

A JEM BOOK

Published by Julian Messner, a Simon & Schuster
Division of Gulf & Western Corporation,
Simon & Schuster Building,
1230 Avenue of the Americas,
New York, New York 10020.
JULIAN MESSNER and colophon are trademarks of
Simon & Schuster, registered in the U.S. Patent
and Trademark Office.

Manufactured in the United States of America.

Design by Regine deToledo

Pictures courtesy of YIVO Institute for Jewish Research

Library of Congress Cataloging in Publication Data

Baldwin, Margaret, 1948-
    The boys who saved the children.

    "A Jem book."
    Adaptation of: Growing up in the Holocaust / Ben
Edelbaum.
    Summary: Ben Edelbaum describes the courage
and strength which held his family together
during the terror of the years in the Lodz ghetto
until they were separated in Auschwitz.
    1. Holocaust, Jewish (1939-1945)—Poland—Lodz
—Personal narratives—Juvenile literature.
2. Edelbaum, Ben, 1928-   —Juvenile literature.
3. Jews—Poland—Lodz—Persecutions—Juvenile
literature.   4. Lodz (Poland)—Ethnic relations
—Juvenile literature.   [1. Holocaust, Jewish
(1939-1945)—Poland—Lodz—Personal narratives.
2. Edelbaum, Ben, 1928-   ]   I. Edelbaum,
Ben, 1928-   . Growing up in the Holocaust.
II. Title.
D810.J4B287   940.53'15'03924   81-14084
ISBN 0-671-43603-1   AACR2

This story is adapted from a remarkable book, *Growing up in the Holocaust*. It was written and published by Ben Edelbaum. This story is true. It is one of many moving accounts in the book of the courage and strength that held one family together. The time was during the terror of the years in the Lodz Ghetto, until they were finally separated, some forever, at Auschwitz.

This book is dedicated to Ben and Dora Edelbaum, two people who have become very special to me. They have taught me a great deal. It is also dedicated to all those who, like Ben and Dora, survived the Holocaust and brought their stories to the world. They are a constant reminder not only of the horror man can inflict upon his fellow man, but of the triumph of the human spirit over the worst horror.

In 1940 the German Nazis rounded up over 270,000 Polish Jews. They herded them into a section of the city of Lodz, Poland. They then sealed this area off from contact with the outside world. It became known as the Lodz Ghetto. Ben Edelbaum and his family survived in this ghetto for four years. Conditions were brutal. The Germans were determined to break the spirit of these people. Already they were destroying them in the death camps. Food in the ghetto was scarce. Ben once saw a young man kill a woman for a loaf of bread. The Germans did not let the people have enough coal to heat the crowded apartment buildings. It was so cold one winter that ice formed on the walls inside Ben's room.

The Jews — men, women, and children — were forced to work long hours for the Nazis. They worked in factories to help the war effort. Only those who could work, and were therefore useful to the Nazis, were allowed to live. The very young, the very old, the weak, and the sick were hauled off to death camps.

CHAPTER
ONE

I CANNOT TELL YOU THE HORROR OF AN Aktion. This means "action" in German. It was the term used by the Nazis when their soldiers came into the ghetto to take away those they felt had no right to live, those who were unfit. Already my older sister, Esther, had been taken. I remember my last sight of her. She stood in a truck in her nightgown with the other hospital patients, afraid, confused. Then the truck drove away. At least she did not see the soldiers throw her newly born infant daughter to her death from the hospital window.

The Nazis would come for us in the night or the early morning. It was always the same. We awoke to sounds of screams and shouts. People ran in panic from street to street, trying to escape. Of course, there was no escape. Little children were dragged from their mothers' arms. Husbands were taken from their wives. Grandparents were torn from their families. Sometimes we heard shots. Maybe the Nazis had caught someone trying to hide. Maybe someone did not obey a command fast enough.

And now, once more, rumors of an *Aktion* had started. Rumors in the ghetto nearly always came true. We had no reason to doubt

this one. And it began. The soldiers moved from street to street. They came closer each day. The day before, they had been in the street next to ours. The next morning, they would come for us.

That night, families from the other apartments in our building gathered in our room. We talked about the coming horror.

"I know they will take him," Rachel whispered. Tears flowed from her eyes. She was looking at her little son, Herschel. The child was six, but he could not walk. He had to be pushed around in a cart.

None of us said anything. What could we say? We knew Rachel was right. Herschel was just the type of person the Germans got rid of. He was a child and useless and a cripple. He had no right to live. But he was all Rachel had left in the world. Her young husband had been one of the first to disappear.

"There must be somewhere to hide him!" my father stated.

"Under the bed?" my sister suggested.

"In the closet?" my other sister asked.

"No," my father shook his head. "Those are the first places the soldiers search when they come into the apartment."

"Then we'll hide him in the open," my

mother said firmly.

We all stared at her. No one spoke. We were all thinking the same thing. My mother was very frail and weak. We were certain that she was in as much danger of being taken away as little Herschel.

My mother walked over and picked up one of the huge sacks the Germans used to give us our skimpy ration of potatoes.

"Get inside," she told little Herschel.

The boy went inside the potato sack without question. Although he was only six, he had been forced to grow up fast. We all had.

"Now," said my mother, "when the Germans come, you must lie very still and not make a sound. Can you do that?"

"Yes," Herschel answered from inside the potato sack.

My mother dragged the sack with Herschel in it near the stove. She draped it to look as if it had just been dumped there. It was perfect. Herschel was just another sack of potatoes!

That cheered everyone up. They began to talk more happily, mostly about food. Food had become the most important thing in our lives. But I soon grew tired of hearing about the different kinds of potatoes everyone had.

How many were frozen or rotten. How many each person got. How they cooked them. Sam and Rita, our neighbors across the hall, came over. I left. I went over to their apartment to spend the evening with Sala.

Sala was near my age. Both of us were about thirteen. She was my closest friend. We had known each other for over a year. We walked to work together, unless she was working the night shift. We waited in food lines together, often for hours. Sometimes I carried her packages for her. That was dangerous in the ghetto. A person who offered to carry your food might run off with it! She trusted me.

Hunger pains often kept us from sleeping. Sala and I spent the long evenings trying to keep our minds off food. We talked about the happy times we had known as children. I showed her the diary I was keeping. She showed me her stamp collection. She had a beautiful singing voice. She sang the sad ghetto songs of our people until tears came to my eyes.

That night, she was terribly frightened.

"Oh, Ben," she said as she saw me, "I know they will take little Herschel. And me!"

She began to cry.

I felt very helpless.

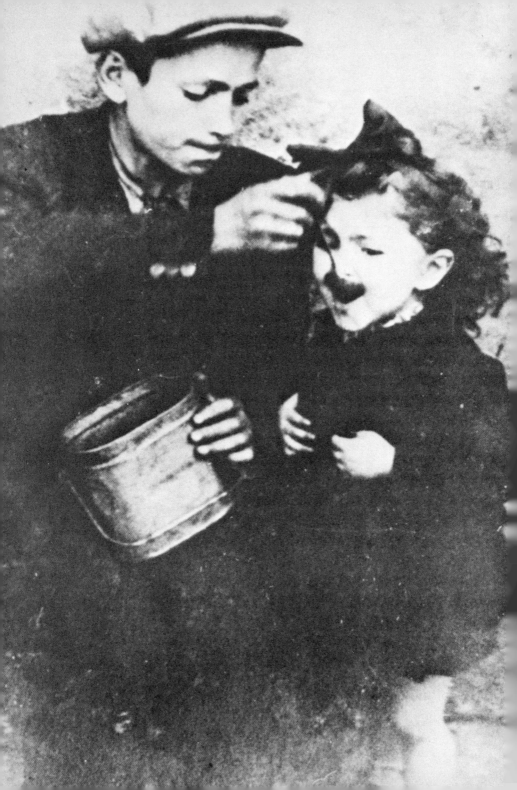

"But if they take you," she wept, "I want to go too."

I walked over to her and took her in my arms. I had never held her before. We sat there, holding onto each other. Then, to my surprise, I kissed her. Through her tears, she kissed me back. I found myself wondering if I would live to be a man. Would I love and marry a woman like Sala?

"Why did this have to happen to us?" Sala cried. "Why were we born now?"

I had no answer. Being together seemed to comfort both of us. Sala stopped crying. She was even able to smile when I had to go.

I returned home. The neighbors had gone.

We all sat quietly, thinking about the terror of the coming morning.

Finally my mother spoke.

"If they take me," she said calmly, "I don't want you to cry and show you are upset. It might make them angry. They might do someone else harm. Just take my food ration and do not grieve for me."

"I won't have you talking that way!" my father shouted angrily. We stared at him, amazed. I had never heard my gentle father raise his voice in anger to anyone, especially not to my mother.

15

He broke down and began to weep. We all did, holding onto each other. We were so tired of the hunger, the cold, the fear.

"Come on, stop this," my sister said. "We better go to bed. We need to look well rested in the morning."

She meant that as a joke, but no one laughed. A good night's sleep and the healthy look it brought could mean the difference between life and death.

CHAPTER
TWO

THEY CAME AT 6:00 A.M.

We heard the screams and shouts. We heard the sound of running feet.

"They're here," someone yelled. "They have already shot a woman. She did not move fast enough when they said to leave the building. They thought she was trying to hide."

My sisters quickly took some beet juice. They dabbed it on my mother's cheeks and lips to make her look more healthy.

Rachel came in with little Herschel. Hurriedly, we put him in the sack.

"Now, my child," she said. She was trying to keep from crying. "The soldiers will come into the room. You must not move or cry out for me. Do you understand?"

"Yes, Mama." Little Herschel was so scared I doubted if he could have made a sound anyway. We closed the sack and left him.

"Everyone out!" came the shouts from the streets. I looked out of my window to see the Nazi soldiers. They had guns in their hands as they walked down the street.

My father began to pray. I wanted to, but the words wouldn't come out aloud. I said them over and over in my heart. We crowded out into the hall. Sala found me. I took her

hand and we held each other tightly all the way down the stairs.

Once in the street, though, Sala and I were torn apart. She was made to stand with her family and I with mine.

We waited while the soldiers went up and searched each apartment. I looked at Rachel. She was white with fear. She had no way of knowing if they had found Herschel and killed him. She could do nothing but stand and wait.

Ten minutes passed.

Finally the Nazis came out. They moved through the crowd, looking at each of us. My heart nearly stopped beating as they came to our family. Their cold eyes swept over us. They passed on.

But when they reached Sala's family, they grabbed Sala and dragged her to the waiting truck. My throat hurt. My heart raced in hatred and anger, but there was nothing I could do. I saw Sam, her father, holding onto her mother. She was close to fainting. The soldiers took two little brothers from their parents, and an elderly woman. Then they left, moving on to the next building. We stood in the street awaiting orders.

The truck drove off. Sala leaned out the back.

"I love you!" she shouted over and over again. "I love you!"

Tears ran down my cheeks into my mouth. I knew she was talking to her parents, but I hoped a little of that love was meant for me.

Finally we were told to return to our homes. The morning work shift was due to report to the factories soon.

Rachel ran up the stairs in a panic. She tore open the potato sack. There sat little Herschel, scared and cramped, but safe!

Until the next time....

CHAPTER
THREE

OUR BLEAK LIVES WENT ON.

Before the war my father had made fur coats. Now he, my uncle, and I all worked in a factory making fur coats for the Germans. When they had forced us to leave our homes, the Nazis had taken all our possessions. They took furniture, money, and clothing, and stored them in warehouses. Our job in the factory was to make new fur coats out of the ones they had stolen from us.

I was foreman in charge of a work group of twelve boys, all about my age. We worked ten hours a day. We had nothing to eat except a bowl of hot broth and coffee. But we boys were very proud of the fact that we were doing grown-up work. It ensured our right to live.

Our job was to cut the fur coats apart and rip out the linings. We had to finish an exact number of coats per day. I got very good at it. I could rip up a coat without damaging the fur in six to eight minutes. I would lay it out, ready to be resewn.

Then, one day, our jobs changed. All the men, women, and children were put to work making white sheepskin coats for the Nazi soldiers fighting on the Russian front.

These coats were very hard to make. Sheepskin is oily. The fur is thick and rough

and clumps together. The Germans used sheepskin because it kept out the snow and the bitter cold. To this day, my thumbs are bent out of shape from pushing the fur back from underneath the sewing machines.

We made hundreds of these coats and shipped them out daily. My boys and I kept up the same pace as the grown-ups. We were very proud of this. We kept telling ourselves that the Nazis must be proud of us too.

Then the white coats began coming back—for repairs.

They were mostly damaged in the same way. There were holes in the front of the coat and even bigger holes in the back. Stained with blood, the holes showed where the bullets had hit. At first there were only a few coats. Then there were more and more. Finally we were working on repairs all the time. We had no news, of course. However, from these coats we could tell that the war was not going well for the Nazis in Russia.

We were ordered to go through the pockets of the coats. We had to bring anything we found to our factory supervisor. We found very little, usually cigarette tobacco. Once, however, we found an arm in a coat sleeve. It had been severed from the body. We

were terribly upset and so was our supervisor. He told the Germans. They came and wrapped it in a blanket in a very solemn ceremony. It was taken away and, we heard, given a military burial. Not long after this, I found a note in the pocket of the coat I was working on.

"May the new wearer of this coat find better luck," it read.

The factory supervisor, Mr Blaugrund, was a very kind man. He did not use his position of authority to take advantage of us, as some did in the ghetto. Instead, he tried to help us. He made our lives as comfortable as it was in his power to do. We thought a great deal of him in return. We did not hesitate to bring our problems to him.

One day, his beloved wife died.

The Nazis had strictly forbidden any type of religious services for us in the ghetto. But every day, after the death of Mr. Blaugrund's wife, we met in secret in his office. He hung a sign on the door that read, "Conference." And every day we said the ritual prayers for the dead for his wife. If the Nazis had caught us, I am sure every one of us would have been shot.

Soon after that, the dreadful rumors started again.

There was going to be another *Aktion.*
This time they were going to take all the children.

CHAPTER
FOUR

As I have said, rumors in the ghetto nearly always came true. They were passed along by those who worked closely with the Germans. Perhaps it was someone in the special Jewish police force that worked in the ghetto who had overheard an officer talking. Soon everyone knew about it. All the children would be taken away. We had little doubt about where they would take us.

My boys and I talked about it as we worked. It was not fair, we decided. At fourteen, I worked next to two grown-up men and kept up with them easily. In fact, I could sometimes do the work better. I was stronger and quicker. Lack of food had not been as hard on me as on the older men.

We knew we had to do something to prove to the Germans we had the right to stay alive. We thought and thought. There was no use in showing them our work. The Nazis would never come to the factory. Even if they did, they would not have been interested. We had to do something to catch their attention.

But what?

The rumors got louder. It was only a matter of time, they said. They would not leave one child in the ghetto.

Every day we talked over different plans.

None seemed any good. We were getting desperate. Then one day one of the boys heard something. The wife of the German officer in charge was going to have a birthday in a few weeks.

"That's it," I cried. "We will give her a present. Something we have made ourselves. Something to show we are hardworking and can do the work of adults. We will make her a fur coat!"

We talked it over. It seemed the only way left to us to escape death. It would be hard. We had just a few short weeks. But at least it gave us hope. It gave us something to do to try to save ourselves.

We went to Mr. Blaugrund and explained our plan. He agreed that it was a good idea. He promised to get permission from the Nazis to use some of the fur in the warehouse to make the coat. Since the coat was not for ourselves, but for a German, the Nazis granted us permission.

We decided to make a Persian paw fur coat. We got Frau Biebow's measurements and began working immediately. We did not have much time.

A Persian lamb coat is made from the fur of the lamb's paws, the most beautiful part.

The fur is short and curly and makes a lovely, swirled pattern. But it only comes in small pieces, no bigger than a lamb's paw. Each piece is about six inches long and two inches wide. These pieces were sewn together by hand to make long panels. There were maybe twenty or thirty pieces per panel. Then the panels were sewn together, again by hand, to make the coat. After that, the lining for the coat had to be made. It was a lot of work. However, we were set on doing it all ourselves. Our fathers gave us advice, now and then, but that was all.

Of course, we had to keep up with our daily work too. We put in our ten-hour shift. Then we worked overtime for several hours. We even took the pieces of fur home at night.

The skin on the fur was very thin and brittle. All the sewing had to be done with tiny, fine needles. If not, the delicate skin would break. It took hour after hour. I often worked by candlelight at night. The Nazis turned off all the electricity at 8:00 P.M. I stitched and stitched, taking tiny stitches until I thought I would go blind. My hands and fingers ached from holding the thin needles.

But at least I was doing something.

The small patches of fur were sewn into

the panels. Then we began to sew the long panels together. This, too, was done with the same tiny stitches. We worked and worked.

All the time the rumors got louder and louder.

We were running out of time.

CHAPTER
FIVE

THE DAY OF FRAU BIEBOW'S BIRTHDAY drew closer. It seemed we would never be finished in time. We began work on the lining of the coat. Our fathers stopped us just as we were about to cut it out. We had come close to making a terrible mistake. We were going to cut the lining smaller than the coat. This seemed logical since the lining would fit inside the coat. But that was not right, our fathers said. The lining must be larger so that it would not bind and pull. It must stretch or the fur part would crease around it.

We cut and sewed for our very lives.

Finally the coat was finished. It was the day before Frau Biebow's birthday. Everyone in the factory, from Mr. Blaugrund on down, gathered to admire it. It was truly a beautiful coat. The panels of lamb's fur swirled in lovely designs. It had to be a beautiful coat. The lives of hundreds of children, we believed, depended on it. It was full-length, with long sleeves and fancy buttons. The buttons were taken from the coats of our people that were stacked in the warehouse. We brushed the coat carefully. Then we folded it up, and put it in a box. But it was not packed until every boy who had worked on it had hung a tag on the bottom of each panel he had sewn. On that tag

were his name, address—and age.

Now, how to deliver it?

This would not be easy. The Nazi High Command was locked away from us in an office building outside the ghetto walls. One had to have a written pass to get by the Jewish police on our side. Then one had to pass the German soldiers on their side.

Mr. Blaugrund agreed to help.

He took me up to his office. His secretary telephoned the central command building. She asked for Commandant Biebow's secretary. We waited. She answered the phone. Mr. Blaugrund motioned for me to pick up the receiver.

My voice shook.

"This is Ben Edelbaum," I said. "Several of us have made a present for Frau Biebow's birthday. I need permission to deliver it to her. May I bring it over today?"

There was silence. I suppose the secretary had to go and get permission from someone else. Finally she came back to the phone and asked to speak to Mr. Blaugrund.

It was all arranged.

Mr. Blaugrund's secretary wrote a pass for me. As foreman, I had been chosen to deliver the coat.

I took the box. Everyone watched me leave.

I walked through the ghetto. Everywhere I went, I seemed to see the children. I saw them waiting in the food lines for hours, for the little bit of food we had to live on. I saw them trudging to work in the factories, day and night shifts, ten hours at a stretch. All of us doing exactly the same work as the adults. I saw the children, their faces pinched with hunger. I saw them and I thought of what we should be doing. Laughing, playing, going to school. I thought of Sala. I knew I would never see her again.

Not one child I passed looked at me and smiled. We had forgotten how to smile, how to laugh. We lived in fear. Fear of not meeting our share of the work load. Fear of having nothing at all to eat tomorrow. Fear of the *Aktion* and the death camps.

As I walked along, I had the strangest feeling that I held the lives of these children in my hands. There was a kind of horror in the thought that the lives of hundreds were sewn up in a Persian fur coat—a gift for the wife of a German officer, made from the fur they had stolen from us.

I arrived at the central command build-

ing. My box and my pass were clutched tightly in my shaking hands.

I could see nothing but walls and barbed wire and closed gates. The Jewish police looked very stern and frightening. And beyond them were the Nazi soldiers.

My courage very nearly gave out. Then I thought of all the long nights of work. I thought of all the children I had seen. I thought of my friends. I thought of Sala.

I handed the man my pass.

CHAPTER
SIX

THE JEWISH POLICE GAVE MY PASS AND ME
a casual glance. Then they called through the
gate to the Germans on the other side. These
men had developed a friendship of sorts from
working together day after day. The Germans
waved me through. I was past the first barrier.

I waited.

Soon a woman in a uniform and high, dark
boots came up to me.

"Are you Edelbaum?" she asked.

"Yes, ma'am," I replied.

"Follow me." She walked into the building. I followed, the coatbox in my hand.

"Sit here," she ordered. I sat on a bench in
front of a room marked Number 3 on the door.
I sat for a long time. People came and went.
They all looked so healthy and well fed! Their
clothes were clean and pressed.

I had put on my best clothes that day.
They were little more than rags, although my
mother did her best to keep them mended and
clean. I felt like a beggar. And, indeed, I was a
beggar. I was a child come to beg for the lives
of other children. Only that morning we had
heard that the soldiers would be coming for us
any day.

Suddenly the door to Room Number 3
opened. Someone came out, I think, but I did

not really notice. Because there, just opposite me, was a picture of Adolf Hitler.

I froze in terror.

I cannot explain the effect the picture of this man had on me. He was the cause of the fear and misery we lived in every day. He was set upon getting rid of us, wiping out our entire race. We had all heard rumors of the death camps, where hundreds, maybe thousands of Jews, died daily. Hitler was just a man, we told ourselves. He was a person like any of us. But in our hearts he had become an evil superman. His picture alone came to represent death and terror. And so the sight of his face pinned me to the bench as surely as if he had run a knife through me.

I longed to run away. But I could not move. The picture stared down at me.

A woman came up and stood in front of me. It was the woman in the boots and uniform. For a moment I was afraid she had come to take me into that room. To him!

I shook with fear.

"Is that it?" she asked, pointing at the box.

I could only nod yes.

"I will see Frau Biebow gets it," she said. She picked up the box and walked away.

Not knowing what else to do, I stood up, turned around, and ran out of that building. Once outside the gate, I felt as though I had been let out of jail. I did not stop running until I had run all the way through the ghetto streets back to the factory.

All the boys were still there.

I had nothing to tell them.

We began to wait.

CHAPTER
SEVEN

FOUR DAYS PASSED.
We heard nothing.
Our hearts sank.

"Suppose she never even got the coat?" one boy said gloomily.

"Suppose she got it and didn't like it?" another asked.

"Even if she liked it," I pointed out, "she may not care about us. Why should she? We are nothing to her."

We grew more and more upset and worried. The rumors about the *Aktion* did not stop.

Then one day Mr. Blaugrund called the thirteen of us into his office.

"Please sit down," he said.

We all sat down on the floor. There were not enough chairs to go round.

Mr. Blaugrund smiled and brought out a letter.

"It is from Frau Biebow," he said. He held it up so we could see it. The letter was written in longhand, by her, personally. He read it to us. It was very kind. She thanked each of us by name for her lovely coat. It was truly a surprise, she said. She was very grateful to all of us for remembering her on her birthday.

Then she had a surprise for us in return. She had recommended that we all be sent to the *Heim* for a week.

We were thrilled!

The *Heim* means "home" in German. It was a special place, outside the ghetto walls. Those who had done special duty or earned a reward in some way were sent there. Three days later, we were all taken there.

Out of the nearly 1,000 days I lived in the Lodz Ghetto, those seven days were the happiest. We slept on beds, on fresh, clean sheets. We were given five meals a day with all the bread and meat and fresh fruit we wanted. I had forgotten what meat and fruit tasted like! I remembered six-year-old Herschel asking his mother what a chicken was. The child had been in the ghetto so long he could not remember.

At the *Heim*, we had nothing to do all day long but play. We were almost children again.

For six days I was very happy. But the seventh was torture. I knew that tomorrow I would have to go back to the fear and the cold and the hunger. But for seven days I had had enough to eat. Later, looking back on that time, I know those days gave us children the energy to go on for at least a few more

months. Many were not so lucky.

On the seventh day I returned to my family. I had missed them and they had missed me. No one was bitter or jealous that I had been to this wonderful place. Our family was very close. My parents worked hard to see that we held onto our love and respect for each other. After all, it was the only thing we had left in life. We had seen what happened to families who lost their love for each other because of the terrible strain of the fear and the hunger. We could hear them at night, yelling and screaming and fighting over food.

My father put his arm around me.

"You have done well, Ben," he said quietly. "The rumors have stopped. We believe there will be no *Aktion.*"

And there was no *Aktion,* at least not for a while.

Was it because of the coat? Did this simple gift prove to the Nazis that we were productive? Did it prove to them that we had the right to live? To this day I do not know the answer. But I like to think that Frau Biebow said a few words to her husband, the Commandant, that spared the children of the Lodz Ghetto for at least a small period of time.

BEN AND HIS FAMILY MANAGED TO STAY TO-
gether in the Lodz Ghetto until it was closed.
Others were not so lucky. Little Herschel was
discovered and taken from his mother. Rachel,
overcome with grief, jumped from a high window in her apartment building and killed her-
self. But when the ghetto was closed, Ben and
his family were herded onto cattle cars and
shipped, with thousands of others, to the
death camp at Auschwitz. Here, as they got
off the train, the Nazis separated the men
from the women. This was the last time Ben
saw his mother and one of his sisters.

Ben and his father stayed together. They
were prisoners at Auschwitz for many days,
waiting their turn to die. Finally they were
taken to the gas chambers. But as they stood
there, a command came through. Their group
was to be taken to a forced labor camp. Here,
however, Ben's father died, unable to with-
stand the terrible working conditions.

The Germans saw the end of the war coming. They saw the Allied soldiers advancing.
The Nazis tried to kill as many of the Jews as
possible. Ben's wife, Dora, who was in Bergen-
Belsen, tells one of the ways they used. Before
the Nazis left in front of Allied troops, they
baked hundreds of loaves of fresh bread and

told the women to eat them. The starving women nearly did so, but a doctor warned them in time that the bread was poisoned.

Ben was put aboard a train, supposedly to be moved away from the danger zone. But the Nazis opened fire on the train with machine guns. They mowed down the Jews crowded aboard, killing hundreds. Ben managed to escape in the darkness, although he was hit in the thigh. A kind farmer took pity on him and hid him for a little while. Ben managed to make it to a road. He collapsed there when he saw a motorcycle approaching. But on the motorcycle was an American doctor who rushed him to a hospital.

The nightmare was over.

Ben was fifteen years old. He weighed sixty pounds.

After the war, Ben found his sister. They were the only two of their large family including aunts, uncles, cousins—to survive.

Out of 160,000 residents of the Lodz Ghetto, only about 1,000 survived the war.

ABOUT THE AUTHOR

MARGARET EDITH (WEIS) BALD-
WIN was born in 1948 in Independence, Missouri. She graduated from the University of
Missouri, Columbia, with a dual degree in Cre-
ative Writing and History. Ms. Baldwin works
for Herald Publishing House as director of the
trade division, Independence Press, and is ad-
vertising director. She has worked for Herald
House for ten years. The author is married to
Robert Baldwin, State Trooper with the Missouri State Highway Patrol,and has two children, David and Elizabeth, and three cats.